For Laura — C.L.

For Bex and Bella — A.P.

First published in 2002 by Macmillan Children's Books
A division of Macmillan Publishers Limited
20 New Wharf Road, London N1 9RR
Basingstoke and Oxford
Associated companies throughout the world
www.panmacmillan.com

ISBN 0 333 76316 5 HB
ISBN 0 333 96226 5 PB

Text copyright © 2002 Claire Llewellyn
Illustrations copyright © 2002 Ant Parker
Paper engineering copyright © 2002 Nick Denchfield
Moral rights asserted

1 3 5 7 9 8 6 4 2

A CIP catalogue record for this book is available from the British Library.

Printed in China

A lift-the-flap life cycle story

Is that a Butterfly?

Claire Llewellyn

Ant Parker

MACMILLAN CHILDREN'S BOOKS

It is a warm summer morning.
In the garden, Snail and Bee
are watching butterflies.

Bee spots something under a leaf.
What on earth is going on?

"Butterflies always lay their eggs under
a leaf," says Snail. "It's to hide them
and keep them safe."
"Will those tiny eggs really turn into
butterflies?" asks Bee.
"Yes," says Snail. "But not right away.
Something else happens first . . ."

About two weeks later,
Bee is flying around the garden.

"Morning, Snail," he buzzes. "Any news
on those eggs?"
"Take a look under the leaf," says Snail.
"You're in for a surprise."

Bee couldn't believe
his eyes. "But those
wriggly things aren't butterflies!"

"I know," says Snail. "They're caterpillars.
Butterfly eggs always hatch into caterpillars.
They're tiny now but you wait and see,
they'll soon begin to grow."

The caterpillars start to eat the leaves and grow bigger every day.

Soon they turn black and speckly and grow yellow spines. Bee spots one of them under the flowers.

"Hooray! I've got prickly spines."

"What's so good about prickly spines?" asks Bee.
Snail smiles. "Well, prickly caterpillars are nasty to eat."
"Aha!" says Bee. "So birds don't like them and leave
them alone."
"Exactly!" says Snail.

The next morning, Snail and Bee
look at the caterpillars again.

Bee looks puzzled. "Why don't they
eat something else?" he asks.
"Those leaves all taste the same."
"It's their favourite plant," says
Snail. "That's why their mum
laid her eggs there."

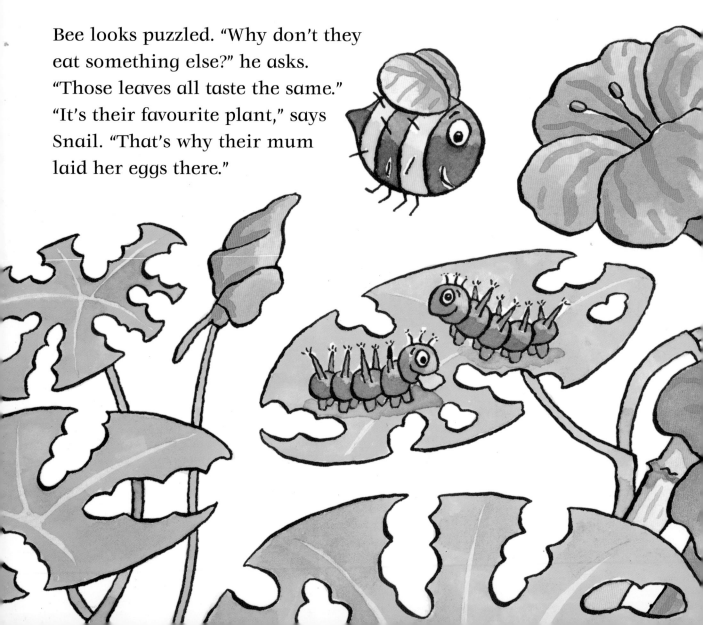

Just then, Snail spots something. "Bee!" he calls. "Quick! Look under the leaf – something funny's going on."

"I knew those caterpillars were eating too much," says Bee. "Nonsense," says Snail. "They all shed their skin from time to time. It's the only way they can grow."

A few weeks later, the garden feels empty.
The caterpillars have disappeared.

"What's happened to them?" asks Bee.
Snail smiles. "This is where it starts to get
really interesting. Take a little look over here."

Bee blinks and stares. "Don't tell me that's a caterpillar? The poor thing. Is it dead?" "Oh no," says Snail. "It's alive inside. That hard case is called a chrysalis. Caterpillars make them when they're fully grown."

"But why?" asks Bee. "Well, something amazing is happening inside," says Snail. "Come back soon and you'll see."

One warm day, three weeks later,
Bee calls over to Snail.

"Quickly, Snail, come here.
Something's happening on this branch."

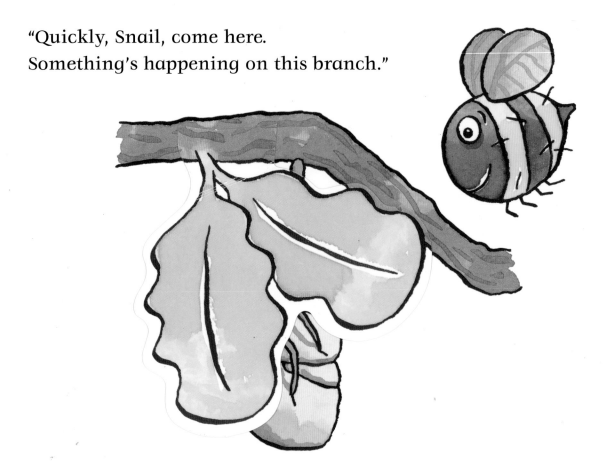

"It's . . . it's a butterfly," Bee whispers.
"I know," says Snail. "First it was a caterpillar.
Then it was a chrysalis. And now it's turned into a butterfly."

The new butterfly rests on the fence and stretches its crumpled wings.

"It's beautiful," says Bee. "Will it fly?"
"Yes, of course," says Snail. "As soon as its wings have dried in the sun."

Snail and Bee watch as the butterfly flutters into the air.

"What will it do now?" asks Bee.
"It will fly off and lay eggs of its own," says Snail.

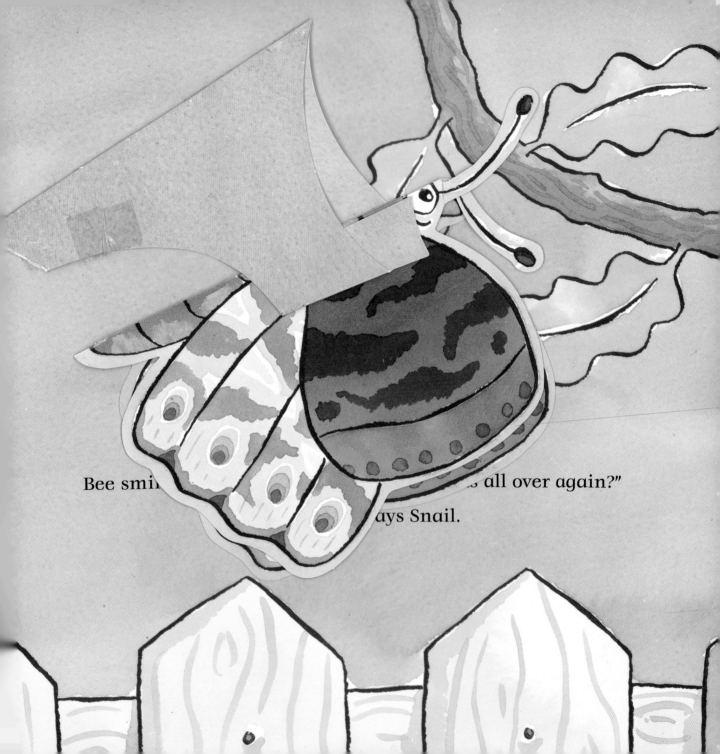

Bee smi... ...s all over again?"

...ays Snail.

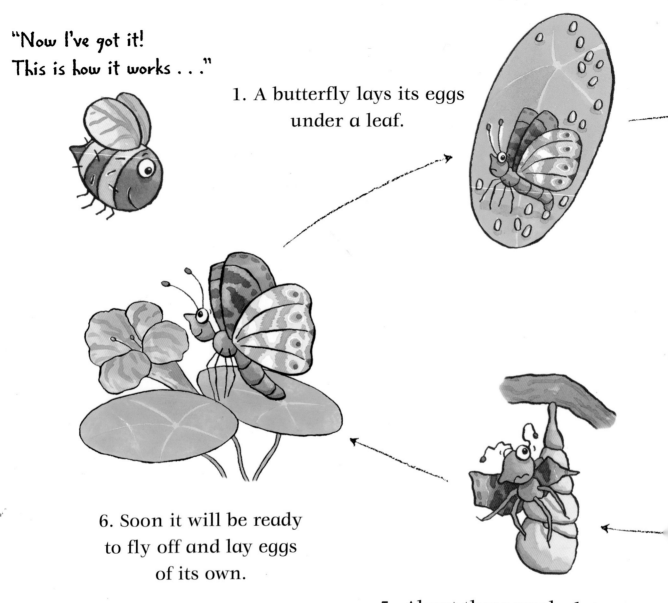

"Now I've got it!
This is how it works . . ."

1. A butterfly lays its eggs under a leaf.

6. Soon it will be ready to fly off and lay eggs of its own.

5. About three weeks later, the chrysalis splits open and a new butterfly crawls out.

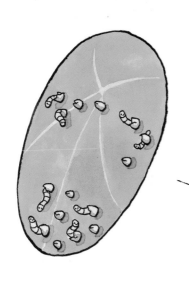

2. About two weeks later, the eggs hatch into tiny caterpillars.

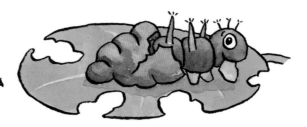

3. They eat and eat and their skins split three or four times as they grow. About four weeks later, the caterpillars are fully grown.

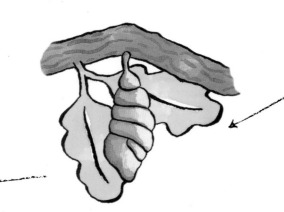

"Aren't butterflies amazing!"

4. They stop eating and make a case called a chrysalis. Inside the chrysalis, the caterpillar's body begins to change.

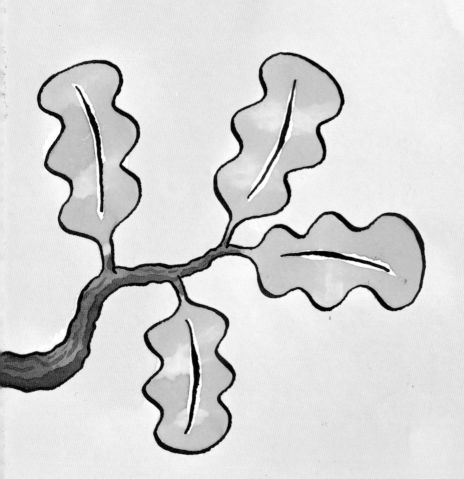